Pet Dog Natural Training

Revolutionize Your Puppy & Dog Training in 14 Days

with these easy-peasy Tips

Micah Jack

Copyright © 2019 Micah Jack

All rights reserved. No part of this publication may be reproduced, distributed, or transmitted in any form or by any means, including photocopying, recording, or other electronic or mechanical methods, without the prior written permission of the publisher, except in the case of brief quotations embodied in critical reviews and specific other non-commercial uses permitted by copyright law.

ISBN: 978-1-63750-248-8

Table of Contents

PET DOG NATURAL TRAINING 2

INTRODUCTION 6

CHAPTER 1 11

    DOGS FUNDAMENTAL COMMANDS 11

        The Heel Command 14

        The Word "NO" 16

        The "Sit" Command 16

        The "Stay" Command 18

        The "Down" Command 19

        The "Off" Command 20

CHAPTER 2 24

    HOW TO EDUCATE YOUR NEW PUPPY OR DOG 24

        LESSONS TO LEARN: 29

CHAPTER 3 38

    HOW TO TEACH YOUR DOG PROPER SOCIALIZATION KNOWLEDGE 38

        Puppy Socialization Do's 40

        Puppy Socialization Don'ts 44

CHAPTER 4 47

    DOG TRAINING/CHOKE COLLARS 47

        The importance of a well fitted training collar 51

        Proper sizing and measurement of the dog for a training collar 52

        Dangers of head collars 54

CHAPTER 5 57

    DOG LEASH & COLLAR TRAINING STEPS 57

        How to educate your dog to accept Collar & Leash 61

        How to Train Your Dog to simply accept its Collar & Leash 66

Training your dog to walk with collar & leash	*70*
Dog leash pulling training	*76*
Dog off-leash training	*81*
CHAPTER 6	**87**
DOG REWARD TRAINING	87
Treats and Food Primarily based Rewards	*92*
The 'Come when Called' Training	*93*
The Use of Reward Training	*97*
ABOUT THE AUTHOR	**102**
ACKNOWLEDGMENTS	**103**

Introduction

Getting a new puppy or dog is usually an exciting thing for any family. There is a good reason why dogs are referred to as people's best friend, and a devoted dog is more than just a pet, it's a treasured member of the family. To reach that stage of affection and companionship, it is far crucial to begin your puppy or dog on the right foot of training.

A strong training in obedience and good manners is vital to making your dog, and you, happier and healthier.

How does your dog sit when you tell it to and mine doesn't?

How can your dog respond to you like that?

"Wow! It comes when you tell it to" - *sounds familiar?*

If it does, you need to make investments into a little bit of primary dog schooling. Start teaching your dog from a younger age because the first few months of its life is when you have the best influence on it; that is when it is formed into the dog it becomes when it's all grown up. The most essential dog education is to get your dog to take a seat and remain calm. Teaching it those commands are crucial for it to get adjusted to. Those instructions are used for numerous unique reasons, if you are in a competition and your dog jumps up and you are unable to make it sit still, this will definitely get him off the competition. To *"come"* is the most primary command. If you take your dog for a walk and you allow it off the leash, you expect it to return back to you and not run around the park with you chasing after it, shouting for it to *"get here right this instant"*. That could be downright embarrassing!

This lesson unites each dog having a forever family. As a vetenary physician, I've shared the wisdom gained from working with various dogs of diverse breed and character to help individuals develop their own pets to well-trained dog that will cause you to feel great about instruction and rewarding your pet with wellness organic dog treats.

This training starts with the fundamentals establishing focus, control and building confidence (trust), and mastering training techniques. Therein, I explain the 6 common commands i teach every dog: *HEEL, NO, SIT, STAY, DOWN, and OFF* commands.

To train your dog the right way to act requires the maximum fundamental techniques; however continuity is essential in its traning. The simplest way to get it to come back is to have a toy on one hand and a treat on the other. When you are in a residential area, stroll a few paces away from it, keep out the toy and call it to you excitingly, when it comes over; supply it a treat, always use the command for come during the duration of the training. Doing this numerous times a day is an exceptional way to educate it, but remember to take lengthy breaks so it doesn't get bored and stop taking part in it, and don't overlook the treats!

Getting it to sit down could be more difficult but again this technnique requires fundamental dog schooling. If you have mastered the *"come" command*, call it to you, place your hand at the tip of its back and say *"take a seat"* at the same time lightly push it down on its backside, while it places its bottom down, deliver it a treat and a number of praises.

In case you want it to sit down longer, just put off giving it the treat and the reward, get it to sit, however take your time bending all the way down to it and feeding it its treat. Basic dog education is straightforward and very powerful. It needs to also be an exciting experience for you and your dog; it shouldn't be an hourly affair daily, merely 5 minutes or so. Don't overlook rewarding your dog and yourself for all the "hard" work!

CHAPTER 1
Dogs Fundamental Commands

There are of course many reasons for dog owners to want a relaxed, obedient and devoted dog.

For one reason, obedient and trained puppies are happier puppies, far less in all likelihood to get into tussles with people or with other dogs.

Another reason is that most neighbourhoods require that dogs residing in their environs be well trained. That is specifically true because lots of breeds tend to have aggressive and behaviorial troubles especially breeds like *pit bulls* and *rottweilers* for instance.

Training your dog nicely will also make it a great

member of the family, especially in households in which there are younger kids. Many researches have proven that proper dog training makes a massive effect when it comes to cutting down the wide variety of dog bites and other behaviorial problems encountered by dog owning households.

While thinking about training your personal dog, or having a personal trainer assist you in teaching it, there are certain fundamental instructions that should be mastered for a dog to be fully trained.

Those simple instructions include:

- **Heel** - It's very important for dogs to stroll beside its owner on a free lead, neither pulling beforehand nor lagging behind.
- **Response to the word "No"** - The phrase "NO" is

one word that every dog must understand. Teaching your dog to respond to this essential word can save you a ton of hassles.

- **Sit down** - Training your dog to sit down on command is a vital part of any dog training application.

- **Stay** - A well trained dog must remain wherein his or her proprietor commands, so; **"stay"** is an essential command in dog training.

- **Down** - Lying down on command is more than just an adorable trick; it's basically a key thing in any dog training program.

The simple obedience commands that each dog have to understand are *"heel", "no", "sit", "stay", "down" and "off"*. These six commands shape the foundation of every fundamental obedience education and it is essential that you and your dog grasp these fundamental commands. These are the fundamentals, and it is going to be difficult to convey into different instructions, or to correct problematic behaviors, without having mastered the basics.

We shall hereby discuss each command sequentially.

The Heel Command

Always begin with the most basic command of all, *the "heel" command.* Teaching a dog to heel is essentially the first step in coaching the dog to stroll nicely while on the leash. The proper region for the dog to stroll is at your side, neither lagging at the back nor straining to get ahead.

If your dog begins to forge beforehand on the lead, gently tug on the leash. For the purpose of training, this will tighten the collar and provide the dog a gentle reminder to fall back in line. If the dog starts to lag at the back, lightly urge him forward. A lure or toy is a great tool for the dog that constantly lags behind.

Once the dog is continuously strolling at your side, try to increase your tempo and encourage the dog to match hits tempo with yours. It must continually be the dog who adjusts his tempo to you; you have to in no way alter your pace to fulfill the wishes of the dog.

The Word "NO"

The phrase *"No"* is a vital one for your dog to analyze, and one that will be useful if you must continue in your dog training. It is crucial that the dog learn to reply to a pointy *"no"* right away and obediently.

The "Sit" Command

The *"take a seat command"* is another crucial training in dog schooling. Teaching a dog to sit down on command, the use of voice instructions alone, will shape the foundation of its schooling, so it's far crucial for the dog to master this vital talent.

The *sit down command* may be mixed with the *heel command*. As you walk alongside your dog, stop all of a sudden. If your dog does not stop when you do, apply a sharp tug on the leash to remind the dog.

Many puppies will instinctively stop when you do, even as others need to be reminded by using **the leash and the training collar.**

Once the dog has stopped at your side, urge him to take a seat by pushing gently on his hindquarters. It's very vital not to use an excessive amount of pressure, or to push it down. Doing so may want to frighten, or maybe injure the dog.

Alternatively, follow a consistent downward strain. Most dogs will understand this as a *take a seat command*. It's far essential to mention the word sit as you do that.

Repeat this process occasionally by means of *strolling,*

stopping and sitting your dog. After a few repetitions, the dog will probably begin to take a seat position on its own each time it stops. It's far vital to mention the word sit down in order for the dog to learn to respond to voice instructions in the long run.

The "Stay" Command

Like the *sit down command*, **the stay command** is an essential and more advanced training. For instance, the stay command is central to teaching the dog to come back which is in turn crucial to off leash strollings.

The *stay command* may be made into an extension of the sit down command. Have your dog taken a seat, and even as it's sitting, slowly move back from the dog. If the dog starts to follow you, as it's in all likelihood at first, come back to the dog and tell it to take a seat once more. Repeat this manner till you can reach the end of the leash without your dog getting up from a sitting position.

After the dog is consistently staying whenever you suggest, you can attempt dropping the leash and backing slowly away. It will probably take the dog some time to stay in a position without moving or getting distracted.

The "Down" Command

The *down command* is another crucial part of any simple dog training command. Teaching a dog to lie down on command is much more than a unique trick. The down command is very essential in regaining control of a dog, or stopping a dog who's engaged in an inappropriate behavior.

The "Off" Command

The *"off command"* is simply as crucial as the other instructions, and it forms the basis for future education, especially while training the dog to stop chasing humans, automobiles, bikes, cats, and so forth.

For example, while training a dog to stay while a bicycle moves away, the proprietor might stand with the dog frivolously at the leash. If the dog begins to stress towards the leash, the owner sharply voices an *"off" command* observed by means of a tug of the leash. Eventually the dog will discover ways to reply to the voice command on its own.

Dog education does tons more than simply to create an obedient, inclined partner. Educating your dog nicely certainly strengthens the bond that already exists among dogs and handler. Dogs are computer animals, and that they look to their computer chief to tell them what to do. ***The key to a successful dog education is to set you up as an absolute leader.***

Setting up yourself as a computer leader is a completely crucial concept for any dog instructor to comprehend. There's always one leader, and the proprietor needs to set him or herself to be the dominant animal. Failure to do so results in behaviorial problems.

A well trained dog will respond well to all of the owner's

instructions, and will no longer show tension, displeasure or confusion. A very good dog training education recognises the importance of allowing the dog to simply do what is expected of it, and could use high quality reinforcement to reward desired behaviors.

In addition to making the dog an excellent member of the family, submission tutoring is a first class routine to meet some of the dog's very own desires, including the need for exercising, the security that comes with knowing what's expected of it, a sense of achievement and a terrific working relationship with its handler. Dog schooling offers the dog a crucial activity to do, and an important aim to attain.

Giving the dog a routine is highly essential than you may think. Dogs had been initially breeded by human beings to do basic activities, such as herding sheep, guarding assets and shielding human beings. Many puppies/dog today haven't had any primary activity to do, and this often resulted in boredom and neurotic behavior.

Primary obedience education, and ongoing training sessions, offers the dog an essential activity to do. This is particularly vital for high power breeds like german shepherds and border collies. Training periods are an outstanding way for these high eccentric dogs or puppies to burn up their extra power and genuinely enjoy themselves.

The art of incorporating playtime into your dog schooling or training sessions is a fantastic way to prevent both yourself and your dog from being bored. Continually have it in mind to play with your dog as it helps to facilitate and reinforce the all-crucial bond between you as the percent chief and your dog.

CHAPTER 2
HOW TO EDUCATE YOUR NEW PUPPY OR DOG

Bringing a new domestic dog into the family is continually an interesting and fun experience. Absolutely everyone wants to play with, cuddle and maintain the little ball of fur. The major thought on the minds of most new pup owners is training the new addition to the family; however it's very important that puppy education and socialization begins as early as possible.

In a few ways; training a puppy is simpler than educating an adult or adolescent dog.

One reason is that the domestic dog is essentially a **"blank slate"**, untroubled through beyond training strategies and other issues.

In other ways, however, the dog may be more difficult to educate than an older dog.

One problem in educating a new puppy is that they are very easily prone to distraction than adolescent and adult dogs. The whole world is new to a puppy, and every new experience creates a new risk and a distraction. For that reason, it's far excellent to keep schooling sessions brief when running with a pup, and to maintain each schooling classes on a high quality level.

Socializing a brand new puppy is a vital part of any education program and it's very crucial for socialization to start early. The window for socialization is very quick, and a doggy that isn't always well socialized to human beings, puppies and other animals especially when it is four months old, by no means develops the socialization it wishes to adopt and end up a terrific dog.

Socialization training is critical to making your new puppy an awesome dog, as dog aggression is a developing problem in many areas. A well socialized dog learns a way to play properly with different puppies, and overly aggressive play is punished by the other puppies in the play organization.

This sort of play mastering is something that takes place amongst siblings in litters of puppies. As the dogs play with each other, they learn what's appropriate and what isn't.

Inappropriate behavior, consisting of tough biting or scratching, is punished by the other dogs, through the mother dog, or both.

Unfortunately, many puppies are eliminated from their mothers and bought or adopted before this socialization has completely come about. Consequently, pup play classes are a completely important part of any puppy schooling education. Most top domestic dog preschool training programs provide time in every session for this type of dog interplay.

Introducing your puppy to new experiences and new places is also an essential part of dog education. Teaching your dog to be obedient and responsive, even in the face of many distractions, is very crucial when educating dogs and puppies.

One wonderful technique to socialise your domestic dog to new humans and new dogs is to take it on a ride to your nearby pet shop and these stores may be incredible places for puppies to get used to new sights, sounds and smells. Of course you will want to ensure the shop permits pets earlier than heading over.

Getting to know the way to interact with other puppies is some thing that generally would arise between littermates. But, since most dogs are removed from their mothers so soon, this littermate socialization often does not finish properly.

One important lesson puppies learn from their littermates and from the mother dog is a way to chunk, and how not to chew for longer periods. Dogs certainly play differently, and their thick pores and skin protects them from most bites. But, when one pup bites too rough, the other puppies, or the mom dog, quickly reprimand it, often by way of keeping hold on the scruff of its neck until it submits.

The high-quality way to socialise your dog is to have it play with multitudes of other dogs. It's also exceptional for the domestic dog to play with a few pet dogs, as long as they're friendly and properly socialized. Many groups have domestic dog playschool and doggy kindergarten

LESSONS TO LEARN:

These instructions can be a terrific way to socialize any domestic dog, and for the handler and domestic dog alike to learn a few fundamental obedience capabilities.

Whilst socializing puppies, it's highly satisfactory to let them play on their own and work out their personal troubles when it comes to seemly rough play. The simplest time the proprietors need to step in is if one dog is hurting every other, or if a severe fight breaks out. Other than that, the proprietors ought to genuinely stand by and watch the dogs interact.

Even as this socialization is taking place, the percentage hierarchy usually turns out to be apparent. Some dogs are ultra-submissive, rolling on their backs and baring their teeths at the slightest provocation. Different puppies inside the class can be dominant, ordering the other puppies around and telling them what to do. Observing the dogs play, and figuring out what sort of character trends your domestic dog has, can be very valuable in determining the best way to continue with greater superior schooling.

As the socialization method proceeds, of course, it will

be essential to introduce the dogs to all forms of human beings in addition to all types of puppies. Luckily, the domestic dog kindergarten style makes this system pretty smooth, because each dog gets to interact with every human. It's very crucial that the domestic dog be exposed to guys, and ladies, antique (old) humans and youngsters, black humans and white people. Dogs do not see each human as the identical. To a dog, a man and a lady are completely different animals.

It's also crucial to introduce the pup to a spread of other animals, especially in a multi pet family.

Introducing the dog to pleasant cat is crucial as with introductions to different animals. The dog may additionally encounter rabbits, guinea pigs and so on. In case your household consists of a more uncommon creature, it's highly crucial to introduce the pup to it as early as possible, however to do it in a way that is safe for both animals.

It is often fine to start by introducing the domestic dog to the odor of the other animal. This may be achieved easily by setting a chunk of the animals bedding, like a towel or mattress liner, near where the puppy/dog sleeps. As soon as the dog is conversant to the scent of the other creature, it is much more likely to accept the animal as just every other family member.

It is very crucial for dog owners to structure their puppy's surroundings in order that the domestic dog is rewarded for suitable behaviors and not rewarded for others. One true example of this is jumping on human beings.

Many human beings inadvertently praise this conduct because it seems cute. Even if it's likely that jumping may be cute for a ten pound pup, it's not going to be so adorable while that domestic dog has grown into a one hundred pound dog.

Rather than praise the dog for jumping, attempt rewarding it for sitting as a substitute. This form of advantageous reinforcement will bring about a well behaved adult dog that could be a valued member of the family and the community at large.

This type of reinforcement can also be utilized in educating the brand new puppy. For example, teaching a puppy to use a completely unique floor including gravel or asphalt is a great method. The idea is that the dog will master this floor and therefore be reluctant to use other surfaces (like your kitchen carpet for instance) as a potty.

It's always first-class to introduce a new puppy or dog to the household especially when the family is calm and stable. This is why animal care specialists discourage mother and father from giving dogs and kittens as holiday presents. The holiday season is usually too busy, with far too many distractions, for a young puppy or kitten to get the eye it deserves. It is nice to wait till the vacations have passed rather than introducing the new member of the family.

Once the puppy is part of the family, there are few matters it must be able to examine. One of the first demanding situations of a domestic dog could be mastering to climb up and down the stairs. Many dogs are afraid of stairs, and that usually means that they do not understand the way to climb them well. It's very critical for the dog's owner to slowly build the self assurance of the dog, taking off at the bottom of the steps. In otherwords, a wide stairway will possibly be much less frightening to the doggy.

To build confidence, the owner should go up a step, and then encourage the dog to join them, using their voice, treats or a toy. After the dog has joined you on the first stair, go back down and repeat the method till the puppy will move up that step on its own. It is essential to build confidence slowly and not to rush the process. Taking it one step at a time is a great way to train the puppy to not be frightened of stairs.

Some other things every new puppy needs to examine is

the way to accept the collar. Gaining knowledge on wearing a collar is vital to every dog, however many puppies are baffled, apprehensive and bewildered via this new piece of gadget. Many puppies continuously try and do away with their new collar through pawing and pulling at it.

Such is vital while choosing a collar on your new domestic dog. A nicely fitted collar, chosen for your puppy's length, is much more likely to be cozy and regular. At the same time a choke, slip and schooling collar may be proper training aids, they must by no means be used alternatively for a sturdy buckle type collar. And of course that collar should have an identity tag and license connected. This identification can be essential in having your puppy again if it becomes separated from you.

The quality and manner to introduce the puppy to the collar is to actually place the collar on and permit it to squirm, leap, roll and paw at the shade to its heart's content material. It's very important to not encourage this conduct with the aid of seeking to soothe the puppy, however it's also just as important not to punish or reprimand the dog.

The high-quality approach is to forget about the puppy and its probable struggle with the collar on. Introducing distractions, including food, toys or playing, is a superb way to get the domestic dog used to the collar. Getting the puppy to play, devour and drink at the same time as wearing the collar is an extraordinary way to get it used to it. After a few days, most dogs will not even remember they are wearing a collar.

CHAPTER 3
How to Teach Your Dog Proper Socialization Knowledge

Teaching a puppy or a dog the right socialization skills is important for the safety of both your dog and other dogs with which it comes in contact. A properly socialized dog is a happy dog, and a pleasure to be around for both human beings and animals. A poorly socialized dog or one without socialization knowledge in any respect is a threat to different animals, other humans or even its own family.

Socialization is easily achieved when the puppy is young and it's very important to remember that the socialization knowledge the puppy learns will have an effect on its conduct for the duration of its life.

A dog that is nicely socialized may neither be fearful nor competitive towards other animals or people. A nicely socialized dog will revel in every new experience and take it in good strides rather than being fearful or competitive.

Puppies that aren't properly socialized often attack because of fear, and such a dog can turn out to be a risk and a liability to the family who owns it. Improperly socialized puppies are also not able to conform to new situations. A recurring activity like a journey to the vets or to a pal's residence can speedily strain the dog out and result in all forms of issues.

Socialization is nicely accomplished when the puppy is very young, perhaps around 12 weeks of age. Even after 12 weeks, however, it's always crucial that the puppy continues its socialization which will refine its all-important social abilties. It's far viable to socialize an older puppy, but it's very tough to gain grounds after the all-essential 12 week period has passed.

There are **do's** and **dont's** when it comes to properly socializing any puppy.

Allow me to start with what to do. Later in this book, we will explore what to keep away from.

Puppy Socialization Do's

- Make all the socialization activities as nice and non-threatening for the puppy as possible. If a pup's first enjoyable experience with any new encounter is an unappealing one, it is going to be very hard to undo that in the dog's thoughts. In some cases, an early trauma can morph into a phobia that can close for an entire life. It's far better to take matters gradually and keep away from having the dog to become fearful.

- Strive to invite your pals over to satisfy the brand new domestic dog. It's always crucial to encourage a specific human interaction and relationship in the puppy's circle of acquaintances, inclusive of men, ladies, youngsters, adults, as well as humans of many numerous ethnic backgrounds and ages.

- Also invite pleasant and healthy dogs over to satisfy your puppy. It's very important for the puppy to interact with a huge variety of different animals, which includes cats, hamsters, rabbits and other animals it is prone to meet. It's also crucial to make certain that each animal the puppy comes in contact with, have acquired all important vaccinations.

- Take the dog to many special locations, along with purchasing centers, pet stores, parks, college playgrounds and on walks across the community. Strive to show the puppy places where there will be crowds of people and plenty of diverse interest taking place.

- Take the domestic dog for brief rides in the automobile. At some stage in these rides, make certain to slow the car from time to time and let the puppy look out the window.

- Introduce your dog to a selection of gadgets that

can be unfamiliar. The puppy needs to be exposed to unusual gadgets like bags, bins, vacuum cleaners, umbrellas, hats, and many others that may be scary to him. Allow and inspire the dog to discover these gadgets and see that he has nothing to fear from them.

- Get the dog used to a spread of objects by rearranging familiar ones. Truely putting a chair the other way up, or placing a table on its facet, creates an item that your domestic dog will perceive as absolutely new.

- Get the puppy used to unusual techniques like being brushed, bathed, having the nails clipped, enamel cleaned, ears wiped clean, etc. Your groomer and your veterinarian with assist with this.

- Introduce the puppy to common matters across the house, inclusive of stairs. Additionally introduce the domestic dog to the collar and leash, so it may be comfy with these objects.

Puppy Socialization Don'ts

There are some matters to keep away from when socializing a dog.

These socialization dont's, consist of:

- Do not abandon the domestic dog on the ground. An assault, or maybe a surprise inspection, through an unknown animal may want to traumatize the domestic dog and hurt its socialization.

- Do not involuntarily praise primarily fear based

conduct. When the puppy indicates fear, it is normal to try and sooth it, but this could encourage the fear based conduct and make it worse. On account that biting is mostly a fear based totally conduct, reinforcing fear can create problems with biting.

- Do not pressurize or rush the socialization system. It is essential to allow the dog to socialize at its personal tempo.

- Do not try to do too much too soon. Young dogs have quick attention spans, and pressing with instructions after that attention span has surpassed may be a waste of your time and your puppy.

- Do not wait too long to begin. There may be a

short window in which to start the socialization system. A young domestic dog is a blank slate, and it is critical to fill that slate with wonderful socialization competencies as early as possible.

CHAPTER 4
Dog Training/Choke Collars

The head collar has become an increasingly more popular dog training system within a couple of years. The mild chief and the halti are the most famous manufacturers of head collar in the market, however there are many different manufacturers of the simple head collar idea.

Many people find the mild chief less difficult to master than the halti, and further the mild chief is designed to lock across the dog's neck. The style of this design is that supposing the dog is in some way capable of wriggling out of the muzzle, it is still wearing a collar. This safety function is very important, especially at some stage in training outside or in novel conditions. On the other hand, the halti gives higher control of the dog, and because of this, it's far often preferred while running with very aggressive puppies.

Training a dog with a head collar has a number of benefits over training with a traditional or schooling collar. For one aspect, head collars are frequently easier to use for starting dog trainers than education collars. Head collars are also pretty powerful at stopping dogs from pulling, or controlling and restraining puppies that have a tendency to pull.

Head collars can also be quite powerful at controlling dogs in tough situations, which includes controlling a dog that wants to be with different dogs. Most owners realize a few situations in which their puppies are hard to control, and head collars may be quite effective at controlling these unstable conditions.

Head collars can be excellent for controlling dogs that are very sturdy, or for running with a dog in a place that includes exceptional distractions. For example, head collars are first-rate for when your dog is on an outing, or in an area where there could be different dogs and different distractions.

Even though a head collar can be a high-quality device, it must not be used as a substitute for powerful dog education. A head collar is simple when it's most utilized in line with sturdy and realistic dog training methods, including reward schooling and other styles of fantastic reinforcement.

The primary dog training collar is known by many names, which include *choke collar, choke chain, training collar, correction collar and slip collar*. These training collars are a number of the popular and most typically used gear with each newbie and expert dog running shoes.

While a training collar is an effective device, like any device it must be used nicely if you want it to be effective for you and secure for the dog. A few of the maximum essential issues when using the training collar are:

- **How the collar suits the dog;** It is essential that the training collar be nicely suited for the dog. A properly geared up training collar is less complicated to use and safer for the dog.

- **Putting the training collar on nicely:** there is a right and an incorrect way to a healthy training collar and if wrongly used, will make it ineffective and probably risky.

- **The proper use of collar:** A training collar ought to be used as a sharp reminder for the dog, not as punishment. It's far crucial that constant pressure be avoided with the use of a training collar.

- **The burden of the chain and the dimensions of the links on the training collar:** It is crucial that the load of the chain be suitable to the size and weight of the dog.
- **The location of the collar on the dog:** It's very essential to properly place the collar on the dog.

The importance of a well fitted training collar

Figuring out if the training collar is the right size is distinctly easy. The precise size of the training collar has to match securely, yet without difficulty over the dog's head. It's very crucial that the training collar should not fit too tightly, however it should not be too free also. A training collar that is too tight can be too difficult to position on. On the other hand, a training collar that is too free can accidentally fall off the dog's head when it lowers its head.

It's also important to understand that a training collar that is too lengthy for the dog requires an amazing deal of finesse to apply nicely. A collar that is too long can nevertheless be used, however it's going to require more ability on the part of the handler.

Proper sizing and measurement of the dog for a training collar

It's very exceptional to measure the dog's neck with a tape line, and then add 2 to 3 inches to the dimension. So if your dog has a neck 12" in diameter, you will need to buy a training collar that is 14" in length. Chain slip collars are usually sized in two inch increments.

While fitting a training collar, the part of the chain that is connected to the leash needs to be on the head of the dog's neck. With this type of arrangement, the collar releases instantly as the leash is loosened. Training collars by design have a way of making the collar tight and free in a quick manner. Tightening the collar is the first part of the correction, and making it unfastened is the second part of the correction.

If the part of the training collar that is connected to the leash is not at the top of the dog's neck, the collar can nevertheless be made tight, however it will not return back to a loose state effortlessly.

The consistent pressure on the dog's neck initiates a counter reaction on the part of the animal, and the dog will quickly learn to pull and stress towards the leash.

In the end, it's far vital to buy a training collar that is

properly made and robust. Buying an excessive excellent training collar, slip collar or choke collar is essential to the safety of yourself and your dog.

If the worst happens, and your dog's training collar does spoil, it's very crucial to not panic. Most puppies might be unaware that they have damaged the collar, at the least for a few minutes. In most cases, in case you act as if the leash remains connected, you could probably get control of your dog again swiftly.

When securing a loose dog, the best strategy is to make a short slip leash by using the snap on the leash and slipping it over the dog's head. It isn't always an excellent approach, but it's going to work.

Dangers of head collars

Despite the fact that head collars have many advantages,

they have a few dangers as well. For one factor, head collars generally tend to make many dogs dependent on the system, and then they quickly examine the difference among their everyday collar and the head collar, and regulate their conduct therefore.

In addition, a few dogs, in particular those not accustomed to wearing a head collar, dislike sporting it and paw at it, try to rub it off or pull excessively. If your dog exhibits this behavior, the pleasant way is to maintain it is to continue till it learns to simply accept the collar. An awesome alternative is to have the dog sit down by way of pulling down at the dog's head.

Any other disadvantage of the top collar is the reaction of many human beings towards it. Many humans assume that a head collar is a muzzle, and react to the dog as if it can chunk. While this is not always a disorder of the head collar, many humans do find it tough.

Dog training with head collars is much like schooling with a training collar or some other device. Whilst the head collar may be a crucial and useful tool, it's very crucial to use it appropriately, comply with all package deal commands, and to combine its use with strong education strategies. The eventual goal of dog education with a head collar is to have the dog behave well with the everyday collar as it does with the specialized head collar.

CHAPTER 5
Dog Leash & Collar Training Steps

There are many specific kinds of dog training, and finding the one that works exceptionally for you is crucial for growing a dog that is a gifted, loyal and devoted member of the family.

All strategies of dog training points to reinforcing the relationship between dog and handler, and the success of a training program is getting the respect of the dog. Fortuitously, dogs are restless by nature so they are looking out for leaders to help them manage the anxiety, and to comply with the direction of those leaders.

Each leash/collar and reward training has been around for a very long time, and have its effectiveness tested over the years. The sort of training that works nicely varies from dog to dog and from breed to breed. It's far vital to keep in mind that every breed of dog has its own specific features, bolstered via loads of years of selective breeding.

Just like human being; the personalities of dogs varies, even within same breeds. You, as the owner of the dog should recognize better than everyone else which style of dog education will work well for your dog, so it's far vital to work with the training you choose to achieve your aim of a motivated, obedient and pleasant dog.

Leash and collar education is an excellent way to accomplish many kinds of dog training, specifically in conditions wherein the dog must have a high level of reliability. For instance, puppies that have crucial activities to do, which includes rescue dogs, police dogs and protection dogs, commonly benefit from leash and collar education.

In leash and collar education, various levels of pressure may be used, ranging from moderate activities with the leash to the very harsh corrections. The measure of correction used must be appropriate to the scenario, considering when the use of an excessive amount of correction, or too little, could be useful or unnecessary.

In a collar and leash based totally dog training application, firstly the dog is taught a selected conduct, typically with the leash. After the dog has been verified that it knows the command, the leash is then used to correct the dog if it disobeys, or while it makes a mistake. *The leash is the principle shape of controlling and communicating with the dog in leash and collar training.*

During the use of leash and collar training, the dog should be trained to believe the handler and take delivery of his or her directions without question. In order for the dog to be completely educated, the handler ought to show the consequences to the dog when it assumes a posture or function she or he does not want it to take. This does not imply the use of pressure; however it does usually require some level of bodily manipulation. This manipulation is most effortlessly and safely accomplished using the principle tool of leash and collar education.

It's far vital for each dog instructor to remember the fact that the leash is absolutely a device. At the same time as the leash is a critical device in this form of education, it is critical for the dog instructor to devise a good way to finally gain the right outcome with the use of some similar equipment available at hand.

Even when the simplest gear at hand is the owner's body and talent, the dog should be willing to obey. Developing a pacesetter/follower courting among handler and dog is still very vital, and it is important to apply the leash as a device and not a crutch. A properly skilled dog ought to be willing to obey whether or not the leash is present or not.

How to educate your dog to accept Collar & Leash

The leash and training collar is the most fundamental piece of device utilized in training a dog. The use of the leash and collar properly is important to successful dog training. The training collar is designed to hold a selected amount of strain every time the leash is tightened. The quantity of pressure placed on the leash controls the amount of strain placed on the training collar, and the stress may be adjusted according to how the dog responds.

How every dog responds to training with the leash and training collar is quite variable. A few puppies barely react the first time they come across a collar and leash, even as others fight this extraordinary contraption with all their might. It's far crucial to recognize how your very own dog reacts, and to evolve your education application as needed.

The first part of training with collar and leash is direction. Getting a high-quality properly-made schooling collar that will direct your dog nicely. There are many kinds of training collars and leashes in the market. The most critical thing is to pick one that is strong and nicely made. The ultimate thing you need to do is chase your dog down after it has damaged its collar. The length of the collar has to be inches longer than the circumference of the dog's neck. It's highly crucial to correctly measure the dog's neck with the use of a measuring tape. With a view to get a correct size, you should make sure that the tape isn't tight around the dog's neck.

Maximum training collars come in even sizes, so that you must measure up to the subsequent size in case your dog's neck is of a typical variety. It is important that the chain that is attached to the collar be placed on the top of the dog's neck. This is where the training collar is designed to assimilate great stress.

The capacity to apply various degrees of strain and to relieve that strain immediately is what makes the training collar such a powerful device. It commonly takes new customers a while to get used to using the training collar, and a few styles of training collar require greater finesse than others. In case you are unsure which collar to opt for, make sure to ask an expert dog trainer, or the management personnel at your neighborhood pet store for help.

After you've become acquainted with the way the training collar works, it's time to begin the use of it to teach your dog to stroll nicely on a lead. The properly trained dog is one that will walk at his owner's side on a loose lead, neither lagging behind nor charging in advance.

The properly trained dog will also vary its tempo to satisfy that of its handler. Under no circumstances does the handler have to be compelled to change his or her pace to fit that of the dog.

If the dog does begin to walk ahead, it is vital to correct the dog right away by giving a quick tug at the leash. This could give the dog an excellent reminder that it needs to change its tempo. It's crucial to quickly relieve the strain as soon as the dog responds. The training collar is designed to relieve stress as soon as the leash is loosened.

Most dog will immediately respond to corrections via an awesome, properly used training collar. If the dog no longer responds as directed, it is crucial to use more pressure. This will be particularly useful for big dogs or the ones who've pre-existing conduct or manipulative problems. In case you are nevertheless unable to get a response out of your dog, it is possible you are using a training collar that isn't big enough for your dog. If you think this could be the case, be sure to seek an expert recommendation earlier.

How to Train Your Dog to simply accept its Collar & Leash

Getting your dog to know how to walk on a collar and leash is the basis of this education for each domestic dog. Till the dog has found how to accept the collar and leash, it will not be possible to perform any extra training.

The first step towards getting the dog to accept the collar and leash is to find a collar that suits the dog nicely. It's very crucial that the collar be neither too light nor too heavy, neither too skinny nor too thick. A collar that is too mild for the dog may be easily damaged, while a collar that is too heavy can be uncomfortable for the dog to put on. It's also crucial that the width of the shade be suitable for the scale of the dog.

Determining the proper length of the collar is pretty cool. Definitely wrap a tape or a string lightly across the dog's neck to get an accurate size. It is vital that the tape measure not be tight, simply roomy.

Most collars are sized two inch increments, so that you may additionally need to measure as much as get a well sized collar. For example, if the dog has a 13" neck, you will buy a 14" collar, and so on.

After you've purchased the suitable collar, the following step is to put it on the dog and allow it to wear it around the house.

Do not be dismayed if the dog whines, paws at the collar

or in any other case attempts to cast it off. That is ordinary; the dog doesn't have to be punished for it. It's far satisfactory to simply ignore the dog and permit it to exercise its own expressions with the collar.

The dog ought to be allowed to wear the collar 24 hours to get used to the feel of the collar on its neck. After the dog has accepted the collar nicely, it's time to start introducing the leash. A lightweight leash works nice for this process.

Likewise attach the leash to the dog's collar and allow it to walk around the house with it. The dog must be supervised for the duration of this procedure if you want to make certain it doesn't get the leash caught on anything. Getting the leash stuck or snagged may want to frighten the dog and create a leash phobia that will be tough to conquer.

At the beginning, the leash needs to simply be connected for a couple of minutes at a time. It is critical to connect the leash at happy times, which include playtime, meal time, and so on.

It's very vital for the dog to associate the leash with glad things. When the leash isn't always attached to the dog, it is a superb idea to keep it close to the dog's meals and water bowls. The dog needs to be encouraged to understand the leash, and to discover that it isn't always something to fear.

After the dog is used to walking round with the leash attached. Allow the dog to stroll around. If the dog bumps into the leash, simply permit it to react and flow as it goes. *The aim of this exercise is to truly permit the dog to get used to the texture of the collar and the leash.* It's always crucial to permit the dog lots of time to get used to wearing the collar and leash before ever attempting to lead it. It is fine to carry out this exercise in the house or different surroundings where the dog feels safe and secure. After the dog is at ease and content on foot on the leash in the house, it is okay to take it outdoors. It's far best to make those out of doors journeys very short at the start, and to extend them slowly over time. Some dogs take to the collar and leash without delay, while others may require additional time.

Training your dog to walk with collar & leash

Walking on a collar and leash is an essential skill that each dog ought to understand. Even the first-class trained dog must by no means be taken outside the house or yard without a strong collar and leash. Even if your dog is skilled flawlessly to go off leash, accidents and distractions do take place, and a collar, with proper identification attached, is the exceptional way to be sure you will get your loved one again.

Of course before you can educate your new dog to simply accept a leash; it should first learn how to spot a collar. The first step is to pick a collar that fits the dog nicely. It's very critical to measure the puppy's neck, and to pick out a collar size therefore. After the collar has been put on the dog, allow it to get used to it. It isn't unusual for a dog to try to tug on the collar, whine and roll or squirm when first introduced to a collar.

The best strategy is to definitely ignore the dog and let him or her get used to the collar. It is a mistake to both punish the dog for gambling with the collar or to encourage the behavior. Distracting the dog often helps, and playing with a favorite toy, or ingesting some favorite treats, can help the dog quickly forget that it is wearing this strange piece of gadget.

After the dog has learned to simply accept the collar, attempt including the leash. Hook the leash to the collar and genuinely sit and watch the dog. Obviously, this ought to most effectively be achieved either inside the house or in restricted outdoor vicinity. The dog should be allowed to pull the leash around on its own, but of course the owner have to maintain a near eye at the dog to make certain that the leash does not come to be snagged or hung up on something.

At first, the leash should simply be left on for a few minutes at a time. It is a good concept to connect the leash at mealtimes, playtime and different high-quality times. That manner the dog will begin to associate the leash with good matters and look forward to it. If the dog exhibits an excessive amount of uneasiness regarding the leash, it is advisable to limit it subsequently to meals times for a while to allow it get used to it slowly. In the end, it's going to come to remember that the leash is not anything to be afraid of.

After the dog is comfortable with strolling around the residence wearing the leash, it's time for you to pick up the leash for a few minutes. You need to try and stroll with the dog on the leash; definitely maintain control of the leash and comply with the dog as it walks round. You need to try and avoid conditions where the leash turns rigid and any pulling or straining on the leash should be avoided. It's problematic for the dog to stay down. Try some video games with the collar and leash. For example, stand up and inspire your dog to stroll in your direction. Don't drag your puppy forward; inspire it to come to you. If it does, praise it profusely and praise it with a meal treat or toy. You must always attempt to make all the time spent on the leash as excellent as possible.

It is crucial to offer the dog plenty of exercise in being used to the leash inside the house. It's very nice to do plenty of work inside the home, considering that it's secure surroundings with few distractions. After the puppy is comfortable on foot inside and on a leash, it's time to start going outside, starting of in small enclosed vicinity like a fenced Yard. After the puppy has mastered walking flippantly outside on a leash, it is time to visit a few places where there are extra distractions. You could need first of all a place like a neighbor's yard. Walking your new dog across the community is a good way to introduce your pals to the new puppy, even as giving the puppy some good petting in fending off distractions and focusing on his leash training.

Dogs ever so often exhibit bad conduct with their leashes, such as biting or chewing at the leash. To discourage this kind of conduct, try applying a bit of sour apple, tabasco sauce or similar substance (simply make certain the substance you apply is not toxic to puppies). This approach commonly convinces dogs that chewing the leash is a bad idea.

Dog leash pulling training

Pulling on the leash is one of the most common misbehaviors seen on all varieties of dogs. Dogs and pet dogs alike can regularly be seen taking their owners for walks, in preference to the opposite custom. Pulling at the leash may be quite more than a stressful dependancy. Leash pulling can lead to getting out of hand situation in the case of a wreck in the collar or leash, and an out of control, off leash dog may be both unfavourable and perilous to itself and to others.

Leash pulling can result from a diffusion of various things. In some cases, the dog may additionally be so excited to head for a walk that it is unable to control itself. In most cases, the dog sees itself as the leader and it truely takes the *"leadership position"* at the front of the dog handler.

If excitement is the incentive for leash pulling, in reality giving the dog a few minutes to relax can frequently be of massive help. Stand with the dog on the leash for a pair of minutes and let the initial pleasure of the upcoming stroll skip. After the initial pleasure has worn off, many puppies are willing to stroll calmly on their leash.

If the problem is out of control, however, a little restraint can be useful. All dog education starts off evolved with the owner setting up him or herself as the alpha dog, or leader, without this simple respect and information, no powerful training can occur. For dogs displaying these kinds of control issues, a step back to fundamental obedience command is necessary. Those dogs can frequently be helped via a formal obedience faculty structure. The dog trainer will of course be sure to educate the handler as well as the dog, and any thorough dog trainer will insist on working with the dog owner as well as the dog.

The idea of coaching the dog to walk calmly on the leash is coaching it to evenly be given the collar and lead. A dog that is bouncing up and down even as the collar is being put on will not stroll well. Start by instructing your dog to sit, and insist that it takes a seat nonetheless while the collar is placed on. If the dog starts to rise, or takes off on its own after the collar is on, be sure to sit it back and backtrack it at once. Best start the walk after the dog has sat and has the collar placed on and continues to take a seat evenly because the leash is attached.

Once the leash is connected, it's very vital to make the dog stroll calmly towards the door. If the dog jumps or surges beforehand, gently correct it with a tug of the leash and get it back to a sitting position. Make the dog stay and then continue again. Repeat this system till the dog is on foot calmly by your side.

Repeat the above method until you reach the door. The dog should not be allowed to surge out of the door, or to tug you by the open door. If the dog begins this conduct, take back the dog into the house and make it sit quietly until it can be trusted to walk through the door nicely. Beginning the walk while in control is important to developing a properly-mannered dog.

As you begin your stroll, it's very crucial to keep the

attention of the dog centered on you at all times. Do not forget, the dog have to look to you for direction, not take the lead itself. When taking walks, it's very crucial to forestall often. Every time you forestall, your dog must stop. Getting into the habit of asking your dog to sit down each time is a great way to keep your dog's interest focused on you. Make certain your dog is looking at you, and then go off again. If the dog begins to surge beforehand, at once forestall and ask the dog to sit. Repeat this technique until the dog is consistently staying at your side. Whenever the dog does what you ask it to, ensure you give it a treat, a toy or simply a reward.

Keep in mind that if your dog pulls on the leash and also you ensure to stop the stroll because you're inadvertently correcting that undesirable behavior. Puppies learn whether or not you're coaching them, and gaining knowledge of the wrong things now will make it difficult knowing the right one. It's far essential to be consistent on your expectancies. Whenever the dog starts to drag ahead of time, without delay stop and make the dog sit down. Remember to have the dog take a seat quietly until its focus is purely on you. Then start out again, ensuring at once to forestall strolling if the dog surges ahead.

Dog off-leash training

Many dog owners worry about giving their 4 legged companions the freedom of going off leash, but it's very important not to hurry that essential step. Puppies ought to be allowed off their leash after they have come to be masters of all of the simple obedience instructions, such as taking walks at your heel, sitting and remaining under command.

Any other ability that needs to be completely mastered before the dog can be taken off the leash is the *'come' command*. Even supposing the dog can heel, sit and live perfectly, if it can not be relied upon to return while called, it isn't prepared up to be taken off the leash.

Taking any dog off the leash, in particular in a hectic, crowded region, or one with a variety of site visitors, is a large step and not one to be taken lightly. It's far crucial to accurately test your dog in safe surroundings before taking it off the leash. After all, the leash is the primary tool of control. You have to be very positive and depend on your voice commands for control before removing the leash.

After the dog has been educated to recognize the take a

seat and stay command, and responds to instructions, it's very crucial to challenge the dog with numerous distractions. It is a good idea to start by introducing other people, different animals, or both, while the dog is in a secure surrounding like a fenced backyard. Have a chum or neighbor stand simply outside the fence while you hold your dog at the leash. Because the friend or family member walks around outside the fence, watch your dog's reactions closely. If it starts off, pull on the leash fast and tug until it returns.

Repeat this exercise until the dog will reliably remain at your side. After this, you may try losing the leash, and ultimately getting rid of the leash and repeating the distraction. It is crucial to vary the distractions, which include introducing different animals, different humans, traffic, rolling balls, etc.

After your dog is capable of staying still in the face of distractions, begin introducing the *'come command'* with distractions in the vicinity. Attempt to invite some of the neighbors, and their dogs over to play with each other. Because the puppies are playing in the fenced yard, try calling your dog. While the dog comes to you, make sure you praise it a lot, and perhaps a meal reward. After the dog has been rewarded, straight away allow him to go playing again. Repeat this several times in the course of the day, ensuring on every occasion to praise the dog and at once allow him to move back to its species.

After the dog has apparently mastered coming when called on its own, strive locating a nearby dog park or similar region where you could practice along with your dog. It's far important to make the location small, or to pick a fenced location incase you lose control of the dog. In case you cannot find a fenced location, pick an area well away from people and cars. Exercise together with your dog by allowing it to play with other dogs, or simply sniffing around, then calling your dog. When it comes to you, without delay praise it, then allow it resume its preceding activities. Doing this may teach the dog that coming to you is the best alternative and the one most probably to bring both rewards and praise at all times.

After the dog has constantly mastred the capacity to come when called upon, even when there are numerous distractions around, it is safe to allow it time without work leash. Off leash time must by no means be an unsupervised time. It's far crucial that you are aware of what your dog is doing at all times. It is simple for a dog to get into trouble fast, so you ought to always keep a fixed eye on it, whether it's chasing squirrels in the park, playing with different dogs, or just chasing a ball with the neighbor's kids.

CHAPTER 6
Dog Reward Training

Reward training is regularly seen as the most cutting-edge technique of training a dog, however reward education is probably a whole lot older than other techniques of dog training. It is possible that reward training for dogs has been around so long as there have been dogs to teach. Early people probably used a few casual kind of reward training when taming the wolf domestic dogs that subsequently evolved into modern-day dogs.

What's called reward schooling or training for dogs nowadays has enjoyed top notch recognition for 10 to 15 years.

Many prized training fanatics are less captivated with different methods of dog training, which include the conventional leash and collar method. However, the satisfactory method for training any dog is often a mixture of leash/collar education and reward training.

Furthermore, a training approach that works flawlessly for one dog can work differently for another, and vice versa. A few dog respond fabulously to reward training and in no way to leash and collar training, at the same time some others may respond to leash/collar education and not feel encouraged by means of reward education. Most dog fall someplace inside the middle of these extremities.

Clicker training is one of the maximum popular sorts of reward education in recent times. At the same time as clicker schooling is not the answer for every dog; it may be a remarkably powerful approach of training many dog. In clicker training, the dog is taught to associate a clicking sound with reward, like a treat. The instructor clicks the clicker when the dog does something good, accompanied immediately with a treat. Ultimately, the dog learns to reply to the clicker on its own.

Most reward training makes use of a few types of meal reward, or a reward that is associated with getting food. In most cases, complex behaviors can easily adopt the use of this type of high quality reinforcement, and you'll find that the individuals who train dogs for movies and television use reward training almost solely.

Reward training is used in all sorts of dog training, along with police and army trainings. Maximum fragrance detection, monitoring and police dog are trained on the use of a few form of reward training. Reward training is also a very powerful method to educate various basic obedience instructions.

Reward training often involves enticing the dog into the

position preferred by the instructor. The lure is used to get the dog to carry out the desired conduct on its own free will.

It makes an excellent deal of sense to get the dog to perform the preferred conduct without any physical intervention on the part of the handler. Getting the dog to perform a conduct without physical contact is vital.

After the dog has achieved the desired conduct, it is given a reward, also known as a fine reinforcement. Treats are often used as reinforcers, but reward, such as "good dog" or a pat on the head, can also be an effective reward.

Having a dog that has been reward trained to be a reliable dog is crucial, especially while the dog has a crucial program, like police patrol or drug detection, to do. Because of this it's far essential to get the dog accustomed to running around in the face of distractions, and to properly socialize the animal to both humans and different animals.

Many dog owners make the mistake of only training the dog within the house or lower backyard, and only while the handler is there. This allows you to end up a reliably skilled accomplice; the dog must be taken outdoors, out of the confines of its protection region and introduced to novel conditions.

It's also crucial to train the dog to take note of the handler always. By keeping your eyes away from the dog means having control of the dog. Reward training could be very powerful at getting the honour and the attention of the dog when used nicely.

Treats and Food Primarily based Rewards

Training with treats and other food primarily based rewards is a first rate way to encourage your dog and speed the training method simultaneously. Most dog are quite motivated by using meal rewards, and most animal schools use this kind of fine reinforcement to train all varieties of animals, together with tigers, lions, and elephants and even residence cats.

It's advisable to start a treat based total training consultation, but it is a good concept to check the dog to ensure that food will motivate him via the consultation. Begin with the dog's everyday supper time by taking a bit of its meals and waving it in the front of the dog's nose. If the dog shows an enthusiasm for the meal, then it's best to start the training. If the dog indicates little interest or none in any respect, it is advisable to do away with the education till some other time. Don't be afraid to put off dinner time for you to pique the dog's hobby in training. The benefits of proper education will outweigh any delay in feeding.

It's very normal to get the dog used to normal feedings, as opposed to leaving food out all the time. Not only does loose feeding encourage the dog to overeat and boom the chances of weight problems, but a free fed dog may in no way be fully prompted in reward primarily based education.

The 'Come when Called' Training

Once your dog has shown interest for the meals presented to it, it's time to begin this education/training. Since you already gave your dogs undivided attention through showing it food, now is a top notch time to start. Deliver the dog some portions of food right away, after which go up again a few steps. While holding the meals with your hand, beckon it with the *"come right here"* command. While the dog comes to you, reward him lavishly and provide him a few portions of meals.

After the dog is coming to you effortlessly, add *"take a seat"* command and maintain the collar before you supply the meals. After the *take a seat* command is mastered, other commands, and even a few hints, may be added. Meals based reinforcement education is the pleasant way to educate a selection of essential behaviors.

One true exercising command is the *take a seat* command. This exercise can start with the owner keeping a foot on the dog, then preventing and asking the dog to sit. After the dog is sitting quietly, the owner backs away and asks the dog to stay. Preferably the dog should continue to stay until called by the owner, despite the fact that the leash is dropped. At the end of the exercise, the owner calls the dog. While the dog goes to the owner, it gets food and reward from the owner. This exercise should be repeated numerous times, until the dog is reliably coming when called.

It's far essential to keep the training sessions quick, especially in the beginning, to hold the dog from becoming bored, and from ingesting its whole meal in the form of treats. After the dog has been responding frequently, the treats and food rewards can be slowly reduced. It's far essential to still offer these food rewards, but don't offer much. After some time, it's not vital to present the dog treats each single time he responds as requested. In essence, it needs to only be essential for the dog to get hold of a food treat one out of 5 instances it comes when commanded. The alternative four successes can be rewarded with praise and scratches.

As soon as the dog is aware of the basics of the *"come right here"* command, the simple command may be improved, and many video games can be created. These varieties of video games may be remarkable fun for owner and dog alike, in addition to a tremendous get to know experience. A few off leash work can be added as well, however it's far more excellent to begin with the dog in a safe surrounding, along with a fenced lower back yard. For variety, you can attempt taking the dog to other secure environments, inclusive of a pal's residence, a neighbor's fenced backyard or a neighborhood dog park. Try leaving the dog free in those safe places, and exercise the come command. Usually praise the dog significantly, scratch it at the back of the ears and tell it what an awesome dog it is. The purpose must be to make coming to the owner a big deal.

The Use of Reward Training

Training dog with the use of high-quality reinforcement and reward training has long been diagnosed as both enormously effective for the owner and a superb experience for the dog. Effective reinforcement education is so essential that it's far the easiest approach used to teach dangerous animals like lions and tigers to work in circuses and within the film and TV enterprise. Proponents of nice reinforcement vouch on the effectiveness of their techniques, and it's far authentic that a good sized majority of dog respond nicely to these training techniques.

One reason why high quality reinforcement training is so powerful is that it makes use of rewards to teach the dog what is expected of it. When the dog performs the desired conduct, it is provided with a reward, most usually within the form of a food treat however it can be a scratch behind the ears, a rub underneath the chin or a pat on the head as well. The crucial aspect is that the dog is rewarded always for doing the right thing.

Reward education has become increasingly popular in recent years, however there are a few sort of reward education among human beings and dog that has been going on for a long time if not hundreds of years.

In understanding what makes reward training so effective, some knowledge of the history of humans and dog could be very helpful. The earliest dog have been likely wolf dog that had been tamed and used by early humans for safety from predators, as alarm structures and later for guarding and herding cattle. It's far viable that the wolf pups that made the best companions had been the most without apparent training, or it's very possible that those early dog were orphaned or deserted wolf pups. Noting their starting place, there's little doubt today that the huge sort of dogs we see these days have their starting place in the wolf.

Wolf packs, like packs of untamed dogs, perform on a strict P.C. Hierarchy. Due to the fact that wolf and dog packs hunt as a set, this type of hierarchy, and the cooperation it brings, is vital to the survival of the species. Every dog is aware of its place in the P.C., and in the event of death or injury, the hierarchy, as soon as set up, hardly ever adjusts.

Each dog, consequently, is highly wired with the aid of nature to look to the P.C. leader for steerage. The basis of every proper dog education, which includes reward based education, is for the handler to set him or herself up as the absolute leader. The chief handler is greater than simply the dominant dog, or the only who tells all of the subordinates what to do. More importantly, the chief gives management and safety, and his or her leadership is essential to the achievement and survival of the pack.

It's far essential for the dog to see itself as part of a P.C., to recognize the human as the chief of that pack, and to respect his or her authority. Some dogs are a good deal less complicated to dominate than others. In case you watch a set of dogs playing for a while, you'll quickly recognize the dominant and submissive personalities.

A dog with a more submissive personality will typically be less complicated to train with the use of fantastic reinforcement, on the grounds that it won't want to challenge the handler for leadership. Even dominant dogs respond thoroughly to high quality reinforcement. There are, in fact few dog that don't reply well to high quality reinforcement, additionally known as reward training.

Fantastic reinforcement is also a nice way to retrain a dog that has conduct problems, especially one which has been abused. Getting the trust and loyalty of an abused dog may be very hard, and superb reinforcement is higher than another training technique at creating this vital bond. Irrespective of what type of dog you're working with, there are possibilities that it can be helped with effective reinforcement training strategies. Base your training strategies on appreciation and reward rather than intimidation and worry, it is the best way to get the most from any dog.

About the Author

Micah Jack is a dog trainer with modern and friendly approach for bringing out the best in all varieties of dog breed. Jack helps you tailor training to your dog's unique traits and energy level; leading to quicker results and a much happier pet.

Acknowledgments

I want to appreciate you for buying and reading this book, likewise my wonderful family, active fans, clients and friends for immense support.

www.ingramcontent.com/pod-product-compliance
Lightning Source LLC
Chambersburg PA
CBHW071020080526
44587CB00015B/2430